S0-BTB-636

MARIE-ANTOINETTE'S VERSAILLES

CÉCILE BERLY

page 1: **Marie-Antoinette's cipher on the wrought iron stairway banister at Petit Trianon**
page 2: **The Hall of Mirrors**
page 3: Élisabeth Vigée-Le Brun (1755-1842), **Marie-Antoinette of Lorraine-Habsbourg**, 1778. Oil on canvas, 223 x 158 cm
page 4: Élisabeth Vigée-Le Brun (1755-1842), **Marie-Antoinette à la rose**, 1783. Oil on canvas, 113 x 87 cm
page 5: **The temple of Love**
page 6: **The Queen's Bedchamber at Petit Trianon**
page 7: Adolf Ulrik Wertmuller (1751-1811), **Marie-Antoinette of Lorraine-Habsbourg, Queen of France, in a riding coat**, 1788. Oil on canvas, 65,5 x 53,5 cm
page 8: **Sèvres porcelain bust of Marie-Antoinette made after a model by Louis Simon Boizot (1743-1809) at Petit Trianon.**

© Éditions Artlys, Paris, 2013
© Établissement public du château,
du musée et du domaine national de Versailles, 2013
ISBN: 978-2-85495-531-6

Foreword

Transcending her tragic destiny Marie-Antoinette has gradually become
a modern heroin. Indeed Versailles was the theatre of the typically
contemporary conflict between private and public life; an issue
that to the 21st century mind was the making – and the breaking –
of many a Royal's life. These palaces – Versailles ruled by etiquette
and Trianon where one sought to escape it – testify to her frantic and
dangerous pursuit of a personal happiness disallowed by protocol.
As Alexandre Maral wrote, "Marie-Antoinette's story resounds as that
of an 18th century Lady Di "lost in translation" in the midst of the Court
of France unable to fathom the hostility surrounding her".
The guide penned by Cécile Berly is much more than a guide
for it reveals the quest of a Queen whose aesthetics, distilled at Versailles,
prevail at Trianon and the Hamlet.
Throughout the rooms where she left her mark a myth takes shape,
that of a sovereign who, in earnest, wished for a life of her own making.

Catherine Pégard
President of the Établissement public du château,
du musée et du domaine national de Versailles

The Chateau of a Queen

Versailles: the most beautiful palace in Europe, created by Louis XIV, the greatest king of France. Marie-Antoinette: the most renowned queen in the history of France; the only queen to have experienced at its fullest the immoderate pomp, splendour and luxury of Versailles; the only queen to have been so tremendously unpopular, hated and ultimately caught in the political turmoil of the Revolution, to have been judged and condemned to a spectacular – though egalitarian – death. Versailles and Marie-Antoinette are henceforth inseparable. The chateau and its grounds bear the stamp of her highness's almighty wishes, not so much in the State Rooms – where absolute monarchy was on stage as sovereign and court alike had to follow strict and constraining rules – but certainly in the Private Rooms where the Queen managed to create an intimate, refined and feminine atmosphere. Though a ruinously frivolous queen of fashion, Marie-Antoinette was also quite probably influenced by novel ideas such as "motherly love", or the benevolence and protection offered by "Mother Nature" as reflected by her earnest involvement in her children's education, and the creation of the domain of Petit Trianon, her favourite place of leisure located at approximately twenty minutes' walk from the palace. Versailles is where the Queen's daily royal representations as mother of the Children of France were displayed in full pomp and regalia according to the rigorous etiquette that prevailed. Versailles and the domain of Petit Trianon also testify to Marie-Antoinette's refined, delicate aesthetics as shown in her private apartments.

Jean-Baptiste André Gautier
d'Agoty (1740-1786)
Marie-Antoinette,
Queen of France, 1775
Oil on canvas, 160 x 128 cm

A
DAUPHINE
AT
VERSAILLES

Arrival at Versailles

Marie-Antoinette's Versailles came late in the chateau's already long history. As the Dauphine and later the young Queen of France, Marie-Antoinette would have to endure for years the constraints of a palace entirely dedicated to the glory of Louis XIV. Indeed, she could have no authority over the administration of the chateau or any influence on politics until she had become the mother of the Children of France.

A political alliance

Married by proxy to Louis Auguste, heir to the throne of France, on 19 April 1770, Marie-Antoinette left Vienna on 21st, after three days of sumptuous wedding celebrations in honour of the sacred union of France and Austria. The journey was exhausting; it took the new Dauphine of France twenty four days to reach Versailles. However, she was warmly welcomed and acclaimed by the people in all the towns she crossed. The royal family met up with her at a clearing in the Compiegne forest. Her grand-father, King Louis XV, was considerate and affectionate, but her husband Louis remained distant and the rest of the royal family (notably *Mesdames Tantes*, the King's spinster daughters) barely concealed their disapproval of any union with the Austro-Hungarian Empire. Though Marie-Antoinette had not yet set foot at Versailles, she was already labelled the "Austrian" and embodied what was considered to be an unholy political alliance.

She finally entered the Versailles courtyard on 16th May 1770, and that very day her marriage was officially celebrated in the palatine chapel. One wonders what could have been the fourteen and a half year old girl's impressions of the Sun King's monumental palace. Had she formed any ideas on such an impres-

❄ *View of the Palace Gates, the Grand Courtyard and the Marble Courtyard*

Joseph Ducreux (1735-1802)
Marie-Antoinette of Lorraine-Habsbourg, then Archduchess of Austria, 1769
Pastel on parchment
64.8 x 49.5 cm

Louis Michel Van Loo
(1707-1771)
**Louis Auguste of France,
Duke of Berry, Dauphin
of France**, 1769
Oil on canvas, 64 x 49 cm

Joseph Ducreux (1735-1802)
**Marie-Antoinette of
Lorraine-Habsbourg,
Archduchess of Austria
and Dauphine of France**,
circa 1770
Oil on canvas, 65 x 54 cm

Claude Louis Desrais
(1746-1816)
**The Wedding Ceremony
of the Dauphin of France
Louis Auguste and
the Archduchess
Marie-Antoinette**,
18th century
Engraving, 37 x 25.5 cm

sive building designed to enable the King of France to supervise and entertain his noble court? Overwhelmed by emotions and the precipitation of the festivities, did she appreciate the beauty of a palace that was considered, and justly so, as the most splendid of Europe? Did she even notice the luxurious décor that set absolute monarchy off magnificently?

On arrival, Marie-Antoinette was quickly shown her State Rooms on the first floor of the chateau looking onto the Midi gardens. They had previously been those of the Queen of France, Marie Leszczynska, wife of Louis XV, who had died in 1768; the apartments had not been renovated since. The chambermaids helped the Dauphine into the court gown made up of impressive panniers under a white brocade dress decorated with a scattering of precious stones and a full-length train. Her hair, neck, wrists and ears were adorned with Crown jewels.

The solemn luxury of a royal wedding

The wedding procession, consisting of the Royal family and dozens of courtesans of the highest ranks, marched to the palace chapel. The church organs announced Marie-Antoinette's entrance, though certainly quite intimidated she maintained her countenance as she joined Louis Auguste, heir to the throne, in front of the altar. The Archbishop of Reims celebrated the marriage; the newly-weds kissed each other clumsily on the cheek then, added their signatures to those of the important members of the Family of France on the registers of Notre-Dame parish. As Marie-Antoinette penned in her given name, ink splattered and a smudge was left on the books. The Dauphine left for her State Rooms where the official members of her Household introduced themselves during a

The Royal Chapel

❋ *The Royal Opera Hall*

long and tedious ceremony consisting of dozens of tributes she had to listen to patiently. These pompous speeches were briefly interrupted by offerings of gifts and precious souvenirs meant to seal symbolically the attachment of the persons now at her service. The magnificence of the celebrations organized to mark the royal wedding was meant to impress European courts. Louis XV and his ministers wished to demonstrate the importance of the Dauphin's wedding, and the pertinence of the 1756 political alliance with Austria, which had so far been strongly and quasi unanimously criticized. Such an immoderate display of luxury aimed to convince of the grandeur of France, of its government, of its King and this, even though the state coffers were empty and the authority of the King was undermined by the open hostility of the parliaments; indeed, Louis XV had long lost the epithet of Well-Beloved King given by the people: his persistent display of libertinage causing an equally consistent disapproval.

In the evening of 16th May, the nuptial dinner, attended only by the members of the Royal Family, took place in the Royal Opera Hall that the King had asked his official architect, Gabriel, to design for the purpose. The décor of the Opera Hall was grandiose: the walls upholstered in blue and silver, the sculptures, mirrors and artefacts were lit up by thousands of candles while an orchestra of eighty musicians added further magic to the festivities. The courtesans

wandered the galleries above as the Royal family dined. Fireworks were planned in the gardens after supper by protocol. However a violent storm put an unexpected end to the rejoicing.

Disappointed, Marie-Antoinette was lead to her room in a very official procession including her husband, the King and a few selected members of court. The *Coucher* (ritual bedding) of the bride and groom was strictly ruled by etiquette. Louis XV gave the Dauphin his nightshirt and the Duchesse de Chartres held out that of the Dauphine. The Archbishop of Reims blessed the bridal bed. Once the curtains were drawn around the newlyweds, the courtesans took leave with a final curtsy. Hence the Dauphine of France spent her first night at Versailles, lying in bed with a perfect stranger who offered her no signs of affection or even attraction to her. The intendants of *Menus-Plaisirs* (bursars in charge of entertainment) had planned nine more days of festivities during which balls, illuminations, fireworks, games, concerts and operas would follow one after the other in a whirlwind of events. Marie-Antoinette overwhelmed by the rejoicings, took pleasure in the sheer luxury, as she had not much been used to this in Vienna.

Jean-Michel Moreau le Jeune (1741-1814)
View of the Royal Opera Hall at Versailles on 23rd May 1770 during the festivities organised to celebrate the Dauphin and Marie-Antoinette's wedding: on stage a performance of Athalie by Racine, 1770
Quill and Indian ink, 25.2 x 29.6 cm

Debut at court

These first wonderful days over, life at Versailles was harrowing for Marie-Antoinette. She hated the palace, its monumental architecture and décor, its "*à la française*" gardens in which nature was as disciplined as were the people in the chateau.

The painstaking apprenticeship of etiquette

Marie-Antoinette could not get used to the obligations imposed by etiquette which she had to learn and accept, and so far did with patience. Having grown up at the court of Vienna in an atmosphere of relative freedom, she just could not comprehend the rituals required by French monarchy. The Hapsburg's were known to live rather simply; Goethe described them as living much like the upper-middle class. The Countess de Noailles, Lady-in-Waiting chosen for her by Louis XV, was in charge of teaching her the strict and constraining rules of etiquette that the royal family had to follow. From awakening to bedtime, their activities were organised so that the courtesans might, at any time of the day, know where to encounter the King and his family in the chateau. Belonging to the Family of France meant belonging to the State. Etiquette did not allow for any privacy.

Marie-Antoinette found these constraining rituals ridiculous. She made fun of the elderly women at court who, caked in make-up, seemed to be congealed figures from the last century. She even voiced her sense of humiliation when, in her official apartments, she had to stand stark naked and wait for many long minutes while her retinue, the royal princesses and one of her step-sisters argued about who should have the right to hand the Dauphine her nightdress according to the strict hierarchical order defined by etiquette. In an attempt to shake the grip of the Countess de Noailles, an emblematic figure at court who took her responsibilities very seriously, Marie-Antoinette nicknamed her "Madame Etiquette". Versailles was quick to spread the new title and the young girl was frowned upon, found to be insolent and disrespectful towards the courtesans. Terribly isolated and bored at court, she had no acquaintances of her own age except for the Princess of Lamballe, a young and melancholic widow. Furthermore she was still confronted with her husband's physical and moral indifference.

Studio of Antoine François Callet (1741-1823)
Marie-Thérèse Louise of Savoie-Carignan, Princess of Lamballe, 18th century
Oil on canvas, 123 x 96 cm

François Hubert Drouais (1727-1775)
Madame the Dauphine Marie-Antoinette as Hebe, 1773
Oil on canvas, 96 x 80 cm
Chantilly, Condé Museum

"The King is dead, long live the King"

During the first days of May 1774, Louis XV contracted smallpox at Petit Trianon. But the King had to die at Versailles. As the illness gradually overcame him, his putrefied face and body began rotting away, within a few days the central building of the palace was filled with an abominable stench. The Dauphin and Dauphine were not permitted to approach the King who was atoning for his sins; so they waited for deliverance in the State Rooms of the Queen. Louis XV expired on 10th May 1774: "The King is dead, long live the King". As soon as the news was officially pronounced, the courtesans all left the *Œil-de-Bœuf* Antechamber and rushed to the new Queen's Rooms in order to pay tribute to the new King Louis XVI.

Marie-Antoinette and Louis XVI were said to have whispered "Please help us, Dear God, we are much too young to reign". Aged respectively eighteen and nineteen, the sovereigns envisaged with apprehension the responsibilities that had befallen them, as they were well aware of how heavy the load was. Louis XVI had, however, been trained from childhood to become King. Though his concerns were both sincere and justified, he saw his role as that of a reformer, a King attentive to his subjects, and wished to restore on all counts the kingdom's reputation, as well as that of France's monarch. The French people were relieved by the death of Louis XV. Indeed his image as a notorious libertine contrasted with that of the young, austere, quiet and hard-working King. Also, Louis XVI absolutely did not intend to afford his wife any political power whatsoever. Hence, Marie-Antoinette was not required to inspire the King in his State decisions; Emperor Joseph II would reproach his sister vigorously and repeatedly for he believed she was not supporting with sufficient conviction and skill the interests of Austria.

Armand Vincent de Montpetit
(1713-1800)
***Portrait of Louis XV
(1710-1774)**, March 1774
Oil on canvas, 74 x 62 cm

The Œil-de-Bœuf Antechamber

THE QUEEN
IN HER
PALACE

Marie-Antoinette's State Rooms

Louis XIV and his architects had planned for the Queen's State Rooms, located on the first floor of the Palace, to be symmetrical to those of the King. The "State Rooms of the Queen of France" consisted of four richly decorated and ornamented reception halls in which the rituals of absolute monarchy were staged. During Marie-Antoinette's time, visitors entered through the Guardroom where the Queen's personal guards watched over her night and day; the 17th century décor was left unchanged. The following room was the Antechamber for the *Grand Couvert* (Official Supper) in which the royal family dined in public. The royal meals were an essential part of the rituals of monarchy and courtesans were eager to attend them. Duchesses, seated on a stool, watched the royal family eat, while the other members of court stood behind them. Marie-Antoinette endured these meals with difficulty, even expressing this publicly once by refusing to take her gloves off at the table, while the King was hungrily devouring his food. The following reception room was the *Salon des Nobles* (Peers' Salon); the Queen had them entirely renovated to her taste: the walls were covered with green damask and the furniture designed with simple refined "*à l'antique*" lines. The ceilings remained as they were.

Antoine François Callet
(1741-1823)
***Louis XVI of France
and Navarre***, 1779
Oil on canvas, 278 x 196 cm

Élisabeth Vigée-Le Brun
(1755-1842)
***Marie-Antoinette
of Lorraine-Habsbourg,
Queen of France and her
children***, 1787
Oil on canvas, 271 x 195 cm

A day in the life of the Queen of France

✿ *The Queen's Bedchamber*

✿ *The Peers' Salon*

✿ *The Antechamber for the Grand Couvert*

✿ *The Hall of Mirrors*

✻ The Queen's Guards Room   ✻ The Royal Chapel   ✻ The Apollo Basin

8 a.m.: *The ceremony of* Lever *(ritual awakening). The Queen is examined by her head physician and head surgeon. Then she prays, washes and dresses following a strictly coded ritual.*

9 a.m.: *Audiences with the Queen. She welcomes into her official apartment courtesans and ambassadors.*

12 a.m.: *Mass at the Royal Chapel.*

1 p.m.: *The Queen lunches in her apartment with a few courtesans.*

Afternoon: *The Queen spends the afternoon at various leisure occupations such as music, theatre, games, promenade, etc.*

7 p.m.: *The Queen dines. This meal is followed by entertainment such as games, balls, performances. Twice a week the Queen dines with the King during the* Grand Couvert *which takes place in the ante-chamber of her official rooms. This ceremony is an inevitable moment in the monarchy's set rituals and is attendant by numerous courtesans distinguished by an invitation extended either by the King or the Queen for a particular public meal.*

11 p.m.: *The ceremony of* Coucher *(ritual bedding).*

The Queen's Bedchamber

Among the State Rooms, the most important room was the official bedroom in which the Queen slept and was joined by the King to conceive the Children of France. She also gave birth there, in front of the royal family and part of the court, to ensure that no stillborn royal child could be substituted for another. The Queen's bed was monumental and ornate, a rich fabric with floral patterns, similar to that of the walls, curtained it; and the canopy was decorated with gilding and further enhanced with huge feather bouquets. At the summit an eagle extends its protective wings. In the official bedroom, either before or during her morning ablutions, she would also entertain the courtesans who had asked for an appointment. Marie-Antoinette did not touch the official décor set by the monarchy and ruled by etiquette; here she bowed to the obligations imposed upon her. The paintings and gilding in the room were produced for Queens Marie-Thérèse, wife of Louis XIV, and Marie Leszczinska, wife of Louis XV. The furniture and chimney are the only things that were change on her arrival; her only personal touch are two medallion portraits, the first of her brother Emperor Joseph II placed over the chimney, and the second of her mother Empress Marie-Thérèse, set on the opposite wall above a large mirror.

Michel Henri Cozette
(1744-1822)
Marie-Thérèse of Austria in mourning, 1773
Tapestry in the Queen's Bedchamber, 95 x 72 cm

Michel Henri Cozette
(1744-1822)
Joseph II, 1773
Tapestry in the Queen's Bedchamber, 95 x 77 cm

❋ *The Queen's Bedchamber*

A modern and loving mother

Antoine François Callet
(1741-1823)
**Charles Philippe of France,
Count of Artois**, circa 1779
Oil on canvas, 70 x 60 cm

Élisabeth Vigée-Le Brun
(1755-1842)
**Yolande Gabrielle Martine
of Polastron, Duchess
of Polignac**, 1782
Oil on canvas, 92.2 x 73.3 cm

As long as the Queen had not become the mother of the *Enfants de France*, she had no political legitimacy within the monarchy and her position at Versailles court remained fragile. Her contemporaries and historians have extensively commented the apparent non consummation of the royal union: how could the King not be attracted to the graceful physique of his wife? Furthermore, how could such a magnificently feminine you ng woman remain faithful to her shy, uninspiring husband and accept his distant attitude for over seven years? The royal couple became parents at last, in December 1778. Following a difficult pregnancy, Marie-Antoinette gave birth to a baby girl named Madame Royale. The young parents though overwhelmed with joy were well aware that the dynasty was not as yet ensured. It was not until the birth of the Dauphin Louis Joseph, in October 1781, that the Queen's growing power would finally be established. In March 1785, the birth of Louis Charles, immediately named Duke of Normandy by the King, and in July 1786 that of Marie Sophie Béatrice, further strengthened her political legitimacy. Nevertheless, pamphlets persistently questioned the King's potency, suggesting the Children of France had been fathered by, for instance, the King's younger brother the Count d'Artois known for his promiscuousness. Accusing the Queen of being licentious implied a comment on Louis XVI's virility. Now a weak, indeed impotent King was believed to be incapable of reigning.

Motherhood enabled Marie-Antoinette to begin exerting a real influence on the King and his political choices. Subsequently her decisions and taste gradually became apparent throughout the interiors of the palace. With the King's authorisation, in 1782, she appointed her friend Madame de Polignac to the prestigious position of Governess of the Royal Children. Under the influence of the innovative ideas circulating on maternal love, and charmed by the image of modern motherhood put forth by the philosopher, writer and composer, Jean-Jacques Rousseau, she demanded that the apartments in the central body of the chateau be reorganised to the advantage of the Polignac family. Thus she could easily visit her children whenever she wished, take part in their education and enjoy sharing their games. By doing this she disregarded etiquette which stated that there should be a marked distance between the King, the Queen, and the Royal Children. Their father was similarly affectionate and concerned. Marie-Antoinette and Louis XVI believed their role as parents had nothing to do with politics. They were first and foremost preoccupied by their children's well-being and individual development, and did their best to preserve them from the constraints of life at Versailles.

Anonymous
The Members of the Royal Family of France surrounding the Dauphin born in 1781, circa 1782-1783
Oil on canvas, 96 x 128 cm

❋ *Door to the Queen's Bathroom in her ground floor apartment*

❋ *Close-up of the wood panels in the Cabinet doré and the Meridian Room*

The Private Rooms

The official chateau of Versailles in which Marie-Antoinette had to live filled her with detestation; she hated the architecture and its ritualised organisation which made it impossible to have the slightest privacy to share a few moments with close friends.

Versailles with Marie-Antoinette's touch

However, once a mother, and particularly when the Dauphin was born in 1781, the Queen could order works to be launched so as to enlarge, renovate and embellish the Private Rooms located at the back of her State Rooms. At last Marie-Antoinette was able to throw herself into interior decorating, revealing her taste and talent at designing luminous though small spaces with the utmost refinement: the dark wood wall panelling was carved with delicate details which set off the furniture and artefacts she loved collecting. The Queen called on the most gifted artists and craftsmen such as the ornamental sculptors Hughes and the Rousseau brothers, Riesener and Jacob the cabinetmakers, Dutemps the gilder, the bronze-smelter Forestier, who were all under the supervision of her architect: Richard Mique, originally from the Lorraine region to the east of France, and previously with King Stanislas. These artists, faithful to the Queen, did not always find it easy to accomplish their tasks. The renovations Marie-Antoinette had commissioned, with the advice of her architect, had to be achieved promptly. It was an immense challenge for the artist-craftsmen to meet the deadlines. Meanwhile the cost of these works was huge and the Queen's Household was consistently in the red. Mique was constantly hunting for additional funding,

Élisabeth Vigée-Le Brun
(1755-1842)
Self-portrait, 1790
Oil on canvas, 100 x 81 cm
Florence, The Uffizi Gallery

which explained in part his conflicts with Count d'Angiviller, director of the King's Buildings, who felt quite justifiably that he was being put in competition with the architect from the east (implying that it was the Queen, and not the King, that promoted the arts at Versailles court.

The *Cabinet doré* (Golden Room)

In 1779, Marie-Antoinette commissioned the first renovation of the *Cabinet doré* (Golden Room), created for Queen Marie Leszczinska it had not been remodelled since. Unhappy with the transformations, the Queen had the wood panels replaced, in 1783, and carved with antique motifs such as palms, sphinx, and trivets which are painted in white and gold; inspired by the latest European fascination: the archaeological excavations in Italy at Pompeii and Herculaneum. Mirrors alternate with the wood panels thus illuminating a room that is considered to be the most beautiful *Cabinet intérieur* (private reception room) of all; it is named after the gilded carved panels and furniture that glitter everywhere highlighting the antique style furniture then in fashion. The Queen welcomed within its walls her closest courtesans and together they enjoyed listening to and performing concerts and recitals. Besides the long hours she spent in the *Cabinet doré* with her "Minister of Fashion", the dressmaker Rose Bertin, she posed there for her official portraitist, Élisabeth Vigée-Le Brun, with whom she had struck up a form of friendship.

Marie-Antoinette and Music

The Queen truly had a passion for music, and this ever since her childhood at the court of Vienna where she met young Mozart; a guest of her mother the Empress. When she was Archduchess, Gluck was her harpsichord teacher. Once in France, she continued her music studies and chose Grétry as harpsichord master — which she also appointed personal music director —, Hinner as harp master and La Garde as singing master. Due to her musical inclinations, and the protection she bestowed upon a number of musicians and composers throughout her reign, she left her mark on late 18th century French music. Her bookcases were lined with a broad selection of her favourite composers' musical scores: Gluck, Grétry, Piccinni, Sacchini, Philidor, Monsigny, Dalayrac etc. She was an enthusiast for opera and invited to France many great European composers; drawing criticism for neglecting French composers. She imposed Gluck on the Parisian public by breaking the rules and applauding at the Première of Iphigénie in Aulide

(1774). She encouraged Piccinni's move to Paris and protected Sacchini. However, in the quarrel between the amateurs of Piccinni and those of Gluck she supported the latter, her countryman, while recognising the talent of his Italian rival. Several times a week, either at Versailles or in Paris, Marie-Antoinette would attend concerts, plays, and operas. She also enjoyed, with the company of her friends gathered in the Cabinet doré, acting and singing some operatic excerpts and arias. On stage, in her little theatre at Trianon, she sang some of the fashionable tunes such as the Devin du village (The Village Soothsayer) by Rousseau (1752). Some pay tribute to her voice, but most find her to be a little off key. The Queen also composed a few songs inspired by ballads.

Jean-Baptiste André Gautier d'Agoty
(1740-1786)
**Marie-Antoinette playing the harp
in her room at Versailles**, 18th century
Gouache, 67.5 x 54.5 cm

View of the Cabinet doré with the harp manufactured in 1774 by the stringed-instrument maker Jean Henri Naderman (1735-1799)

✽ *Detail of the bronze ornaments by Pierre Auguste Forestier (1755-1835) in the Meridian Room*

The *Cabinet de la Méridienne* (Meridian Room)

The renovation of the *Cabinet de la Méridienne* (Meridian Room) was launched in 1781 when Marie-Antoinette was expecting her second child and hoping to give a dauphin to France. This private room is particularly small and offered the Queen a refuge during her moments of midday respite. The Queen could rest alone without being disturbed even by her servants as she could lock the door from the inside thanks to interior bolts stamped with her cypher "MA", which had been added. These bolts are decorated with hearts pierced by the royal fleur-de-lis sceptre, symbolising the King protecting his Queen's rest. The wood panels of the octagonal room are painted white and gold and punctuated by large mirrors (which enhance luminosity). The alcove, set in between two wall panels, is upholstered in the same blue silk fabric used for the curtains and the furniture, and complemented with mirrors. Sculpted bronze ornaments decorate the woodwork and the mirrors with dolphins, which symbolise the birth of an heir to the throne, while other motifs and emblems speak of the Queen: her feminine taste (roses in bloom) and her imperial origins (eagles with their bludgeons caught in branches).

❋ *View of the enfilade leading from the Queen's Private Rooms to the Œil-de-Bœuf Antechamber*

The *Cabinet du Billard* (Billiard Room)

In addition to enlarging the bookcases in the library – which she crossed on her way to either the *Cabinet doré* or *Méridienne* –, Marie-Antoinette requested that a Billiard Room be installed on a mezzanine located on the second floor right above the *Cabinet de la Méridienne*. She had a billiard table set up there, as it was a game she enjoyed playing with her closest circle of friends. The décor testifies to her taste for the charming "*tapissier*" style upholstery which blends a profusion of floral and vegetal patterns caught in ribbons and bows. One of the Queen's favourite cabinet-makers, Georges Jacob, designed the furniture. In the Billiard Room she kept a magnificent jewellery box, a gift from her grand-father Louis XV on her wedding day. Made of precious woods and decorated with delicately painted porcelain fitted into sculpted gilded bronze, the jewellery box was filled with dozens of fine accessories, precious stones and pearls which belonged to the late Dauphine, mother of Louis Auguste.

Near the mezzanine room, the Queen had a few other tiny rooms furnished, including a room upholstered in a painted linen fabric called *toile de Jouy*. Marie-Antoinette loved these sweet little rooms that she decorated with great pleasure using a wide variety of beautifully refined objects: clocks, curios, lacquered pieces, porcelain vases (the bouquets were changed daily), perfume dispensers, chandeliers, sculpted busts and other fashionable Chinese objects.

Martin Carlin (circa 1730-1785)
Marie-Antoinette's jewellery box, 1770
Rosewood, sycamore, gilded bronze, soft-paste Sèvres porcelain framed by an ornate floral decor of green and gold painted bouquets,
95 x 56 x 36 cm

❋ *View of the* **Cabinet du Billard**

***Box in the shape of a small
dog lying on a low table***,
18th century
Wood, maki-e décor, black
and gold lacquer, Japan,
15.5 x 23 x 12.7 cm

Spendthrift

The Queen's taste for the frivolous was also apparent in her almost compulsive need to buy jewellery and diamonds, purchases her personal coffers could not afford. She therefore requested help from the King who obliged without the slightest remark, and paid off her creditors. Marie-Antoinette, the spendthrift Queen, had yet another "vice" since she often wiled away her afternoons, evenings and even nights gambling. Indeed, a number of games (cards, billiards) were highly fashionable at Versailles and throughout the aristocratic milieu in Paris. Nobility and wealthy Parisians alike were going bankrupt and ruining their families due to their addiction to gambling. The Queen's Household organised several times a week the Queen's Games, in the *Salon de la Paix* located on the first floor of the chateau, next to the official bedchamber of the Queen. Card tables were set up to welcome the game enthusiasts. Marie-Antoinette favoured *Pharaon* and *Lansquenet*, losing tremendous amounts and accumulating debts. Again she had to ask for the King's personal financial support which he usually offered happily despite the royal ban on gaming implemented to fight usury.

❁ *Services stairs for the water-bearers*

❋ *The Queen's Bathroom*

The ground floor apartment

In 1782, at the death of Madame Sophie, one of the King's aunts, Marie-Antoinette took possession of her three room apartment on the ground floor of the chateau, at the rear of the Marble Courtyard, to which she had access through the service stairs from both her private and State Rooms on the first floor; thus she could commute unbeknown to anyone but her servants. The bedchamber of the apartment was refurbished without delay and completed before the end of 1783. The following year she commissioned a bathroom from Mique, her architect; the wood panels create a simple but elegant water environment: sculpted swans quench their thirst in ponds, surrounded by dolphins, reeds, shellfish, pearls and coral branches. These motifs are painted in white delicately contrasting against the light blue colour of the panelling. Shortly before the Revolution, she had the bathroom paved with large black and white marble tiles. Next to the copper tub a resting bed was set up: ever since her childhood in Vienna, Marie-Antoinette had been used to bathing regularly and delighted in such moments of peace and quiet, during which she sometimes took a light breakfast consisting of a coffee or a chocolate.

It was the first time that, at Versailles, the Queen had been given a double private apartment in the palace, as the King of France had. She could live there undisturbed, alone or in the company of her close circle of friends. The courtesans, however, voiced loudly their disapproval of such exorbitant spending for the Queen's sole pleasure and that of the obscure lesser nobility living off her. But worse was the fact that the Queen felt she could bow out of her duties towards etiquette, depriving the court of her presence. The general opinion was that the Queen's lifestyle was quite simply scandalous.

The Queen of Fashion

During the first years, Louis XVI supported his wife's enthusiasm for fancy clothes. She had barely become Queen and was already passionately involved with fashion to such an extent that she was both the "Queen of fashion" and considered to be the very first muse of the history of design. The origin of such a consuming and costly passion was her meeting, in the gardens of Marly, with the milliner Rose Bertin; introduced to her by the Duchesse de Chartres. At the time, Rose Bertin had been enjoying an extraordinary ascension both socially and economically. The dressmaker, born in the country of the Picard region, had come to Paris at sixteen to work in a milliner's shop as a needlewoman. But Rose Bertin's creativity, style, strong personality and business sense resulted in her opening her own shop in 1770: "Le Grand Mogol" on Rue du Faubourg-Saint-Honoré. She would soon employ over thirty young seamstresses and work with a broad array of at least one hundred and twenty suppliers. Rose Bertin travelled several times a week from Paris to Versailles, finally even renting a house in town. She visited the Queen at Versailles not, however, in her State Rooms — absolutely forbidden by etiquette — but in her private rooms and more often in the Cabinet doré. There, she would unfold her marvels before a thrilled Marie-Antoinette: the latest fabrics, her newest designs, novel accessories and extravagant reproductions. A perfect courtesan, Rose Bertin skilfully guided the Queen in her choices as the latter attempted to imagine her own designs. Together they truly initiated a series of sartorial revolutions. The court found it highly inappropriate that Rose Bertin should claim she was "working with Her Majesty" as her "Minister of Fashion", while Marie-Antoinette encouraged her dressmaker, pushing her to design clothes for the European and French elite so that her creativity would not abate. They both intended to free the female body from the often painful constraints of formalwear: the stay was now only worn for ceremonial events; materials were becoming lighter and often

vaporous like the dress that scandalised the court at Versailles and in Paris — described as "en gaulle" — worn by Marie-Antoinette in a renowned painting by Élisabeth Vigée-Le Brun. Marie-Antoinette is Rose Bertin's muse: everyone's eyes were on her therefore she was a showcase for French know-how and fashion design.

Léonard Autier, the hairdresser, and Rose Bertin made up the wildest of teams. Together they imagined "poufs": immoderately large, eccentric, overblown hairdo's that could reach up to over a yard in height. These were given names such as "to independence", "to sentiment", or the famous "Quès aco Marin"; they were vast hair constructions including all manner of objects and vegetation generally highlighted with pink, white or blue feathers. The pair had an enormous influence on Marie-Antoinette. Their closeness —one might even say intimacy— with the sovereign was widely disapproved of at court as, despite their creative genius, these commoners had the gall to rule

over what was worn by the Queen and henceforth the ladies at court and the Parisian elite. Furthermore this fashion rage caused the ruin of many a French family that could not keep up with the constantly changing and increasingly expensive trends.

Claude Louis Desrais (1746-1816)
Marie-Antoinette Queen of France in formal dress, 18th century
Engraving, 31 x 21 cm

Anonymous
Commemorative hairdo called Independence or the Triumph of Freedom,
circa 1778
Coloured engraving, 33 x 24.8 cm
Blérancourt, Franco-American Museum
of Château de Blérancourt

THE DOMAIN
OF MARIE-
ANTOINETTE

Petit Trianon,
a Country Palace

Originally, Trianon was the name of a village bought by Louis XIV with a view to building a chateau for his leisure; a place where he could rest, far from court and its constraints; a private hide-away for his adulterous love affairs. In turn, Louis XV, on Madame de Pompadour's suggestion, had his architect Gabriel build an exquisite little cube-shaped chateau of pure and classical lines called "*à la grecque*". With reference to the Sun King's Grand Trianon, impressive for its size and remarkable pink marble peristyle, it was named Petit Trianon. The renowned royal "*favorite*" would never enjoy the edifice as she died, in 1763, just a year after the works had been launched. As soon as the construction was completed, Louis XV elected Petit Trianon as his preferred country house. He would stay there with his latest official mistress, Countess Du Barry, whose well-earned reputation for voluptuousness spiced with sensuality the remaining years of his reign. It was at Petit Trianon that Louis XV caught small pox which led to a frightfully long agony and finally his death. At court and throughout the Kingdom, the chateau was associated with the disorderly private life of a libertine King who had forsaken the duties of a Christian life and the constraints of etiquette.

The advantages of Petit Trianon did not, however, escape Marie-Antoinette. The young Queen, only a few days after their grand-father's passing, informed Louis XVI that she wanted the chateau for herself; indeed she could easily imagine living there on her own terms, away from court, in the company of friends of her choice and a small staff of servants. Hence the King offered her the royal palace and, on 15th August 1774 – on Virgin Mary's day –, he gave her a master key for the Petit Trianon set with five hundred and thirty diamonds by the jewel-

❋ **Petit Trianon façade,
view from the parade
grounds**

Élisabeth Vigée-Le Brun
(1755-1842)
**Queen Marie-Antoinette
wearing a white muslin dress,
described as "en gaulle",**
1783
Oil on canvas, 90 x 72 cm
Darmstadt, Schlossmuseum

✻ *Medusa head sculpted in 1765 by Honoré Guibert (1720-1791)*

Anonymous
Portrait of Count Axel de Fersen, 18th century
Plate, 25 x 17 cm
Blérancourt, Franco-American
Museum of Château
de Blérancourt

ler Maillard. Thus the Queen had become the owner of a royal palace. This was unheard of in the history of absolutism, and caused the very first scandal of her reign, as a queen – even more so a foreign queen – was not permitted to own French patrimonial holdings. Marie-Antoinette could not care less. Grateful and happy she would dispose of the Petit Trianon and its gardens. Considered to be a masterpiece of the budding neo-classical style, she hardly touched the architecture of the palace made up of four distinctive yet perfectly balanced façades.

On the ground floor, the vestibule opens on a large stairway with a richly decorated banister of wrought iron and gilded bronze: Marie-Antoinette's cypher ("MA"), woven into the sculpted bronze replaced that of Louis XV ("LL"). The flight of stairs leads to the first floor of the chateau. On the landing, between two windows the large and terrifying Medusa head was carved by Honoré Guibert in 1765. In 1784, the Queen decided to have the billiard table taken upstairs from the room – then called the Billiard Room– next to the Guards' Room. The magnificent billiard table was replaced by a much simpler one for the guards. The ground floor was also equipped with a *réchauffoir* where the dishes, prepared in the service building next door, could be reheated before being delivered to the Queen and her guests; henceforth keeping any persistent kitchen smells from invading the delicate interiors.

The "gentle life"

Life as Marie-Antoinette perceived it at Petit Trianon was to be pleasant, simple and as private as possible. She shared the facilities – and her time – with a few friends chosen, not because of their aristocratic titles or the honourable ranks held at Court but because of their personalities and taste for the "gentle life" often associated with the 18th century. In addition to the

Vestibule at Petit Trianon, view of the wrought iron and gilded bronze banister by François Brochais (18th century)

❋ *View of the first (noble) floor antechamber at Petit Trianon with the Élizabeth Vigée-Le Brun (1755-1842) portrait*
Marie-Antoinette à la rose

Polignac's and their circle of friends, Count Fersen was often present at Petit Trianon and Marie-Antoinette's benevolent attitude towards him did not go unnoticed. The Queen also particularly enjoyed the company of her youngest and unwed step-sister, Madame Élisabeth, who was very religious; she stayed on the attic floor in rooms that were originally meant for her brother Louis XVI (who never wished to sleep there). The Royal Children were of course welcome, Madame Royale, the eldest daughter, had a room on the attic level.

On the first storey of the chateau, in the main dining room (the small one had become the new billiard room), the Queen organised dinner parties. So as not to be interrupted by the servants during his gallant meals, it was believed Louis XV used the much commented on "flying tables"; these, however, never did exist. In the reception salon, Marie-Antoinette's circle of friends spent their time at conversation, gaming, needlework and, first and foremost, listening to or playing music. The Queen was adamant that protocol should be banished from her palace: when she entered a room her guests were requested to continue their activities without acknowledging her.

Anonymous
Élisabeth Philippine Marie Hélène of France, known as "Madame Élisabeth",
18th century
Oil on canvas, 62 x 52 cm

Élisabeth Vigée-Le Brun
(1755-1842)
Marie-Thérèse Charlotte of France and her brother the Dauphin Louis Joseph, 1784
Oil on canvas, 132 x 94 cm

❋ *The Salon de Compagnie*

The Sliding Mirror Room

Running on from the reception salon was the Queen's bedchamber. Originally Louis XV's private study, it was taken over, in 1772, by Countess Du Barry, his mistress. The "ears of wheat" furniture was commissioned by the Queen from one of her favourite cabinet-makers, Georges Jacob; the woodwork was carved with flowers, garlands of leaves, ears of wheat and pine cones. The seats were upholstered with woollen fabric woven with floral and vegetal motifs illustrating an idealised natural environment. Next to her room she had a small boudoir set up called the Sliding Mirror Room. These mirrors were ordered, in 1776, from the engineer Mercklein. The room was specially fitted for the mechanisms that enabled the mirrors to slide downwards or upwards, thus closing off the two windows that opened on to the terrace from which the Queen could admire her gardens (and notably contemplate the temple of Love); when the mirrors are up their reflections bounce off one another.

✳ *Marie-Antoinette's cypher sculpted in the wood panels of the Sliding Mirror Room*

Rumours and discredit

Besides the high cost of the delicate mechanism, the court was scandalised by the very existence of such a room where the Queen could, whenever she wished, isolate herself entirely. No sooner had she taken possession of Petit Trianon than the first *libelle* was circulated titled "*Le Lever de l'aurore*" (The Break of Day), in which she was lampooned for the inappropriate liberties she took such as watching the sunrise in the company of unruly and inconstant young men. Once again Petit Trianon was, in the collective imagination, associated with debauched royal behaviour. Marie-Antoinette was seen as a licentious queen that could not be bothered with her duties of representation and despised the courtesans. The court felt directly insulted by the strict instructions she had posted upon the gate to her domain, stating that "by order of the Queen" no visitor – including the King – may enter uninvited. With Bonnefoy du Plan, the superintendent at Petit Trianon, she drew up a list of guests; to these guests Bonnefoy would give a token: *Jetton de la Reine* (the Queen's token) was inscribed on one side and on the obverse the arms of France and Austria were intertwined. It did not take long for Petit Trianon to be renamed "Little Vienna" or "Little Schönbrunn", labels that greatly hurt the Queen if we are to believe the *Memoires* of her First Lady-in-Waiting Madame Campan who of course, due to her function, had a room at Petit Trianon.

Though the court probably scorned the Queen's behaviour without real reason, Marie-Antoinette certainly did nothing to prevent the rumours; she even increased her visits to Petit Trianon. Worse, when, in 1779, she fell ill with the chicken pox, she decided to stay at her chateau during her illness and convalescence with four of her circle of friends to play nurse: Messieurs Besenval, Coigny, Guines and Estherazy; the first three, at least, had an established reputation for libertinage.

Queen's token, 1785
Bronze, 36 cm

Joseph Boze (1744/1745-1826)
***Portrait of Jeanne Louise Henriette Genet,
wife Campan***, 1786
Pastel, 81.2 x 64.4 cm

❊ *Views of the Queen's Bedchamber and its "ears of wheat" furniture onto the gardens and the temple of Love*

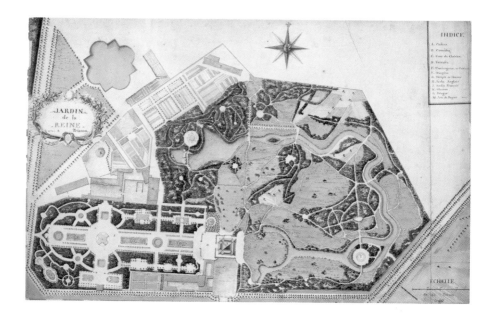

The English gardens

Marie-Antoinette often referred to Petit Trianon as "my garden". Indeed, the Queen had a veritable passion for gardens and their arrangement. From that point of view she was in complete harmony with the tradition established by Louis XIV – and continued by Louis XV – of creating entire décors of greenery. As with her other interests, Marie-Antoinette was taken by the latest fashions in the art of landscaping. Under the influence of the philosophers of Enlightenment, and Jean-Jacques Rousseau in particular, the elite idealised unspoiled Nature as being healthy and invigorating, good and benevolent towards mankind. The "*à la française*" gardens designed during the previous century by Le Nôtre had fallen out of favour for they subjected Nature to geometric rules, obliging it to become perfectly symmetrical. The latest trend was clearly English.

In the "*à l'anglaise*" gardens Nature was landscaped so as to appear to have grown at random. Rivers would cut their way in twists and meanders along the grassy grounds to fill artificial lakes that had to look as natural as possible. Trees and flowers, whether rustic or exotic, were planted in a carefully unplanned pattern. Their heady scents greeted the walker as they rounded a steep hill; while exploring these paths one would discover environments that were designed to resemble those of high mountainous ranges. Landscape ornaments such as ruins, small temples and "*à la grecque*" buildings, reminiscent of an imaginary Orient and the recently rediscovered Antiquity were being built. By exalting both Mother Nature and history, these "*à l'anglaise*" gardens were a pre-Romantic environment conducive to solitary wanderings and daydreaming.

Jean-Ernest Heinsius
(1740-1812)
Richard Mique, 1782
Oil on canvas, 65 x 54.5 cm
Nancy, Musée Lorrain

Thomas Malgloire Daussy
(18th century)
***Layout for the Queen's
Gardens at Petit Trianon
as was from 1780 to 1785***
Water-colours, quill, 46.7 x 73 cm

Richard Mique and his assistants

As early as August 1774, Marie-Antoinette had the initial works on the gardens launched, under the supervision of her architect, Richard Mique, who immediately gathered a new team around him including: Hubert Robert, the painter of ruins and Antoine Richard, the son of Louis XV's gardener, who was obliged to follow the architect's instructions. The Queen also requested advice from an amateur gardener, Count de Carman, whose most perfect "à l'anglaise" Parisian gardens had absolutely entranced her. The Count swiftly produced some drafts that she handed to Mique to approve. The first step involved levelling part of the French garden located under the windows of one of the Petit Trianon façades in order to install there a – no longer existing – Chinese themed carousel (jeu de bague) featuring dragons and peacocks. The Queen similarly had Louis XV's hothouses destroyed; the plants – including a large amount of extremely rare species – were transferred to the King's Paris gardens (the current Jardin des Plantes). She had that site landscaped to resemble the steep and rocky Alp Mountains. The entirely artificial "Escargot" (snail) mountain was completed with a waterfall, a river and two ornaments the Rock and the Grotto – for which it took no less than seven drafts before pleasing the Queen. The Duke de Cröy, an accomplished gardener and an enthusiast for French gardens, wrote in his Memoires: "Instead of the great hothouses (which were the most scholarly and expensive of Europe), some quite high mountains, a large rock and a river. Never has a couple of acres changed to such an extent nor cost as dearly."

Claude Louis Châtelet
(1753-1795)
View of the carousel from the gallery and one of the Petit Trianon façades, 1771
Water-colours
Modena, Biblioteca Estense

✿ *View from the top of the "Escargot" mountain onto the Rock and the Belvedere*

❋ *View of the Domain from the bridge leading to the Rock*

The bridge and the Rock

❋ *Inside the Grotto*

The Grotto

The completely artificial Grotto illustrated the prevailing taste for a pictu-resque vision of nature, inspired by the philosophy and Romanesque works written by Rousseau such as *Julie or the New Heloise* (1761) and *Reveries of a Solitary Walker* (1776-1778). Hidden within a wild and quite inhospitable natural environment, one had to travel narrow bramble and high grass lined pathways which became muddy with the slightest rainfall. Once inside, a mossy stone bench rewarded the weary rambler. Though this ornament might seem quite innocent, it too caused a scandal; indeed the Queen could see without being seen through a slit made between the rocks for that very purpose. Should she spot an undesirable visitor, she could then disappear through a screen door. As a matter of fact it is said that Marie-Antoinette was inside the Grotto when, on 5th October 1789, she was warned by a letter from Saint-Priest of the march of Parisian women onto Versailles.

The temple of Love

Marie-Antoinette also had a number of small temples and buildings constructed in her gardens; they were all in the ancient Greek style. The very first was the temple of Love, built from 1777 to 1778, on a small isolated island carved out by the river. It is a masterpiece of neoclassical architecture by Richard Mique: designed as an open temple topped by a flat cupola set on twelve Corinthian columns with marble capitals and friezes sculpted by Deschamps. The temple harbours a copy of a remarkable piece by Bouchardon *Love Carving a Bow in Hercules's Bludgeon* (1750) produced by another great 18th century sculptor, Louis Philippe Mouchy (the original sculpture is kept at the Louvre Museum). The temple of Love was magnificently staged during the great *fêtes* organised by the Queen. In 1781, when Emperor Joseph II visited for the second time (he had come to Versailles incognito the first time in 1777), Marie-Antoinette organised a grandiose party for her much loved and yet feared brother (she was afraid of his disapproval). Over six thousand four hundred faggots of wood were cut to be burned in a trench dug behind the temple of Love, the fire illuminating it as if by magic. Thousands of Chinese lanterns and candles in terra-cotta bowls were spread around the grounds, lighting up the trees and the flowers adding to the fairy-tale atmosphere. This *fête*, as well as the one held, in 1782, in honour of the Great Duke Paul of Russia and his wife – who travelled under the name of Count and Countess of the North – left an extremely vivid impression on all those who were lucky enough to attend because of the ephemeral luxury deployed.

Eugène Battaille (1817-1875), after Adolf Ulrik Wertmuller (1751-1811)
Marie-Antoinette of Austria, Queen of France, with her first two children, 1868
Oil on canvas, 275 x 188 cm

Louis Nicolas de Lespinasse (1734-1808)
View of the temple of Love in the English gardens at Petit Trianon, 1780
Water-colours, gouache, 21.5 x 35 cm

❈ *The temple of Love and* **Love Carving a Bow in Hercules's Bludgeon** *by Louis Philippe Mouchy (1734-1801) after the version by Edme Bouchardon (1698-1762)*

Dome of the temple of Love by Joseph Deschamps (1743-1788)

The Belvedere

Just a little after the works had been launched for the temple of Love (1777), the construction of the Belvedere was initiated at the top of the artificial mountain inspired by the landscapes of the Swiss Valais region. Richard Mique designed an octagonal pavilion and entrusted once again Deschamps with the exterior decorating; the latter created four low-reliefs illustrating the seasons of the year as well as the ornamented pediments. He also produced the eight female sphinxes that are arranged round the terrace. The Belvedere was completed in 1781. The high windows cut out in each of the sides of the perfect octagon offered the Queen a panoramic view of her grounds. The interior is decorated with delicate stuccos painted with arabesques and animals – fish, squirrels, and little monkeys – garlands of ribbon trimmed white roses, bouquets unravelling, quivers and bows. The ground is paved with white and red marble tiles. Marie-Antoinette and her friends would listen to musical performances there while enjoying refreshments.

Expensive facilities

The expenses incurred by the many works and landscaping at Trianon were excessively high and some years outrageously exorbitant (the Queen would be highly criticised for these during her trial in October 1793). Marie-Antoinette could not settle these amounts on her own budget. As she had grown accustomed to, she would request the King's help; he, in turn, would order the amounts to be paid out of the State budget. On 22nd August 1775, 100 000 pounds were entered on the Royal Treasury books "for the Queen's gardens". Such extravagant expenditures solely for the pleasure of a small set of people shocked both the court and the nascent public opinion.

Claude Louis Châtelet
(1753-1795)
Illumination of the Belvedere Pavilion and the Rock, 1781
Oil on canvas, 59 x 80 cm

The Belvedere

❋ *Inside view of the Belvedere*

❋ *Exterior view of the Queen's Theater*

The Queen's Theatre

Marie-Antoinette had a passion for the theatre, comedy and the opera. As a child she had sung, danced and acted on stage with her brothers and sisters. She kept fond memories of the wedding of her eldest brother, the future Emperor Joseph II, in January 1765, during which, with her siblings, she had had the opportunity to display her talents in the ballet *The Triumph of Love* at Schönbrunn palace. In fact, she had the painting titled *Representation of the Ballet, The Triumph of Love, at Schönbrunn during the wedding of Joseph II on 24th January 1765* by Georg Weikert hung at Petit Trianon. Sometime before leaving Vienna for France, to perfect her French accent, she had rehearsed short scenes with two French actors. And in the greatest secrecy, as Dauphine, she had acted in a few scenes of the French repertory (*Les Précieuses ridicules* – The Affected Ladies), with her young brothers-in-law the Counts de Provence and d'Artois and their wives, before one single spectator, the Dauphin – who usually dozed off before the end of the play. When she was queen, the actors of the *Comédie-Française* and those of the *Comédie-Italienne* performed each week at Versailles for the royal family. She would even frequently travel to Paris to attend performances.

The chatelaine of Petit Trianon was, therefore, eager to organise theatre entertainment at the chateau. To begin with she demanded that a temporary stage be set up in the Gallery of Grand Trianon (1775). Then she had the theatre moved to Louis XV's Orangery (1776-1777). At last, in 1778, she asked her architect Richard Mique to build a small theatre house on the former site of a Louis XV greenhouse. Her future theatre required a theatre company so she created the Company of Lords the main members of which were Count d'Artois, the Polignac couple, their daughter and step-son, the highly dramatic Diane de Polignac, Vaudreuil (Madame de Polignac's lover), Estherazy and Adhémar.

Attributed to Georg Weikert
(1745-1799)
Performance of the pantomime-ballet **The Triumph of Love,** *at Schönbrunn during the wedding of Joseph II on 24th January 1765*
18th century
Oil on canvas, 288 x 211 cm

❀ *View of the stage at the Queen's Theatre*

A small theatre for high society

Mique studied the Choisy theatre and of course the Royal Opera Hall at Versailles. He presented the Queen with a coloured wax model that included lighting, drapes and silk curtains. She immediately approved the sketch and ordered that it be built with diligence. From the outside the theatre looks like a small antique temple. The façade is plain and could even be overlooked among the lime-trees of the French Garden. Two feminine figures, sculpted by Deschamps, stand guard in the theatre vestibule. The first is Melpomene, the Muse of singing, musical harmony and tragedy; in her left hand she is holding a sceptre, in the right a dagger. The second is Thalia, the Muse of comedy; she is accompanied by a cherub and carries her attributes in each hand: a flute and a mask. The sobriety of the exterior contrasts greatly with the interior of the theatre, though of small proportions it is a delicate and extravagant gem for its rich ornamentation. Shaped as an inverted and slightly flared U, the sculpted decorations once again entrusted to Deschamps are made of gold and blue

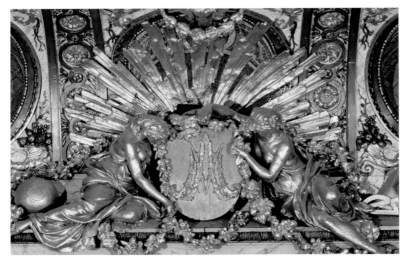

❋ *Close-up view of the sculpted woodwork at the Queen's Theatre showing Marie-Antoinette's cypher*

coloured pasteboard on a background of veined faux-marble. The "*tapissier*" (upholstery) style of the décor borders on tacky due to all the ribbons, garlands, bows, golden tassels, fringes, drapery and crowns pierced by arrows, flowers, plants etc. The gilding commissioned from the painter Boquet, is a mixture of gold and copper. The caryatids at each side of the stage edges seem to be emerging from the drapes. In the foreground two trophies, also in movement, are carrying candelabras. The entirely wooden mechanisms backstage are remarkable; a masterpiece of engineering they allow for rapid backcloth and décor changes. The oval ceiling painting, *Apollo, Melpomene and Thalia with the Graces*, is a work by Lagrenée le Jeune. Oculi (circular windows) support the ceiling. In June 1779, the Crown's embroiderer, Tremeau, delivered a magnificent stage curtain that he managed to manufacture in less than a month. According to the historian Pierre de Nolhac, the total cost of the theatre came to 141,200 pounds. It was completed sometime in 1779 and inaugurated on 1st June 1780. For the occasion the Company of Lords performed two short plays including *La Gageure Imprévue* (1768) by Sedaine an author the Queen appreciated immensely, and is now forgotten.

An inappropriate inclination

Though Marie-Antoinette was not much of a reader – she even found reading rather boring – she managed with enthusiasm the Company of Lords. She chose the plays for the repertory, distributed the roles, ordered the costumes, supervised the set and organised the rehearsals. To help her in this she was assisted by two professional actors, Caillot and Richer, whom she generously compensated. The works she preferred were generally short and entertaining, the plot often consisted of young girls of common descent,

innocent farm girls, taken advantage of by evil and powerful Lords. The Queen took on the leading parts, mostly naïve servants or overly sentimental maids. Apart from Sedaine's plays, Marie-Antoinette also presented the one act opera written in 1752 by Rousseau, *Le Devin du village* (The Village Soothsayer), in which she played the role of Colette a milkmaid. The performances where usually interrupted by short musical pieces (*ariettas*).

Yet again, the Queen's activities caused scandal. Her taste for the theatre contributed to her increasing unpopularity. The Company of Lords performed before a small and select group of spectators: the Trianon servants by obligation, the King, a few members of the royal family and a number of courtesans handpicked by the Queen. The court was not invited and therefore indulged in commenting profusely the fact that the Queen of France was exposing herself and flaunting her "*favoris*" on stage, while performing parts which questioned social hierarchy… the epitome of impropriety! A Queen who playacts – terribly of course – the roles of a farm girl or a milkmaid could only be a wolf in sheep's clothing who respects neither her rank nor her blood, a debauched "*favorite*" of the King. The coup de grace landed in October 1785, when the Lords performed *The Barber of Seville* (1775) in the presence of Beaumarchais, the author. Marie-Antoinette played the role of Rosine and the Count d'Artois that of Figaro. The play had been censured ten years earlier by the King for its subversive message. Undoubtedly the contents had been toned down as indeed the Queen would never have dared perform a play struck by the King's prohibition without filtering out the most seditious passages. Also, Beaumarchais had undoubtedly selected excerpts from his lengthy text to propose scenes that could be handled by amateur actors – which they all were except for Count de Vaudreuil who was deemed the greatest society performer of his time –, nevertheless the scandal was tremendous; amplified further by the revelation of the Affair of the Queen's Necklace a few hours before the first performance began. To put a stop to the outcry the Queen had no choice but to disband the Company of Lords and put an end to her theatrical activities.

Pierre Paulet (1896-1978), after Jean-Jacques Lagrénée le Jeune (1739-1821)
Apollo, Melpomene and Thalia with the Graces and Pheme riding Pegasus, and amorini carrying garlands of flowers, ceiling of the Queen's Theatre, 1968
Oil on canvas, 776 x 583 cm

The Affair of the Queen's Necklace
(1785-1786)

On the morning of 15th August 1785, after an Extra-ordinary Council held in the King's study, the Cardinal de Rohan was arrested in the galerie des Glaces (Hall of Mirrors) and, by a signed order of King Louis XVI (lettre de cachet), imprisoned at the Bastille. Madame Campan revealed the whole affair: the jeweller Bœhmer had complained to her about Rohan defaulting payment on the purchase of a neck-lace on behalf of the Queen. Rohan indicated those who had instigated the swindle: Madame de La Motte-Valois, a poor descendant of a bastard, though legiti-mised, son of King Henri II; her husband Monsieur de La Motte, an obscure officer faced with enormous debts; and their accomplice Rétaux de Villette, a former comrade in arms and an accomplished counterfeiter. To these colourful characters was added the charlatan occultist Count de Cagliostro who, a priori, had not taken part in the swindle but held sway over the Cardinal de Rohan by reassuring him on his future. The Queen's animosity towards Rohan certainly impeded his ministerial projects. Madame de La Motte who, in the name of her ancestry, claimed to be a cousin of the Queen organised for him a secret reconciliation with a Marie-Antoinette impersonator, a prostitute from Palais Royal named Nicole Le Guay; the meeting took place nightly, sometime in August 1784, in the Bosquet of Venus in the Versailles gardens. La Motte then convinced Rohan to purchase on behalf of the Queen, in the utmost secrecy, a necklace unique of its kind and outrageously expensive, the famous "collier à l'esclavage", originally created for the Countess Du Barry, that the Queen had refused seve-ral times, despite Louis XVI's offer to purchase it for her. Rohan accepted and delivered the necklace to Madame de La Motte. The La Motte couple then took the necklace apart and sold most of the diamonds in England.

The whole kingdom was wrought up by the resounding trial that further besmirched the name of the Queen. The Cardinal and Nicole Le Guay were acquitted. Count de La Motte and Réteaux de Villette were condemned to a life sentence of hard labour. Madame de La Motte was branded with the letter "V" —for voleur: thief in French— on both shoulders and jailed for life. She, however, managed to escape in broad daylight from the prison of Salpêtrière and find refuge in England from where she inundated France with pamphlets blaming the Queen and accusing her of all the country's woes, clai-ming the Queen was evil: a Sapphic and manipulative conspirer, with a unquenchable thirst for gold and the people's blood. According to Goethe the affair of the necklace "is a direct preamble to the Revolution".

Facsimile of Marie-Antoinette's necklace assembled by Charles Auguste Boehmer and Paul Bassenge, 18th century. Reproduced in zircon, 45 x 38.5 cm

Jean-Baptiste Letourmy (circa 1774-1812)
Portraits of the protagonists involved in the scandal of the Queen's necklace, 1785
Plate. Paris, Bibliothèque nationale de France

LOUIS RENE EDOUARD
Prince de Rohan Guemenée Cardinal de la S.te Egl. Romaine

JEANNE DE SAINT REMY DE VALOIS
Epouse du Comte de la Motte

M.R LE COMTE DE LA MOTTE

M.lle DE LA TOUR

M. LE COMTE DE CAGLIOSTRO

SERAPHINA FELICHIANI
Comtesse de Cagliostro

M.lle LE GUET DESIGNY DOLISVA

M.r BETTE DETIENVILLE

M.me MELLA DE COURVILLE SULBARR

M.r LE BARON DE FAGES

LA FEMME DE CHAMBRE
de M.me la Comtesse de la Motte

LE PERE LOTH
Minimes

Se trouve à Tours et a Orleans chez les S.rs l'Eleurmy libraire

The Hamlet and the Farm

The Hamlet is a life-sized theatre décor. Marie-Antoinette satisfied her fancy for the picturesque by imagining the small Normandy village with Richard Mique; made up of a group of twelve houses – landscape ornaments – with purposely cracked walls, and thatched rooftops. Works were launched, in 1783, on a site extending the English Gardens. The Hamlet was designed to be a secluded area where one could enjoy the – factice – pleasures of a rustic country life as imagined by the upper crust in the late 18th century. Farm life, as described and idealised by Rousseau, was fashionable and several aristocrats of royal descent sought to reproduce this, however with a refinement far from any reality. Prince de Condé was the very first, from 1774 to 1775, to have a hamlet built on his grounds at Chantilly. Although Marie-Antoinette had probably never read Rousseau she was enthralled by the result.

Around the Queen's House

The Hamlet is established around the Queen's House consisting of two distinct buildings: to the right, the Queen's cottage, and to the left the Billiard house. Both ornamental edifices are set on the eastern banks of the large lake (excavated and sealed with clay in 1784). They are linked by a wooden gallery decorated with flowers (geraniums, wallflowers, hyacinths) planted in white and blue ceramic pots bearing the Queen's cypher: "MA". On the ground floor of the Queen's cottage there are a large paved dining room and a games room (backgammon was a favourite). Under a Mansard style roof, the top floor housed the Queen's rooms: a large reception room, a small living room and a Chinese study. The ground floor of the Billiard house consisted of a billiard room and two cloakrooms (one for men the other for women), and on

Claude Louis Châtelet
(1753-1795)
*View of the Hamlet with
the lake in the background*,
from *Recueil des plans
du Petit Trianon*, 1781
Water-colours
Modena, Biblioteca Estense

The Queen's House

❋ *The Marlborough Tower*

The Queen's House from the Marlborough Tower

❋ *View of the wooden gallery linking the Queen's cottage to the Billiard Room*

❋ *View of the Queen's cottage seen from the wooden gallery on the first floor*

the upper level a small apartment probably used by Richard Mique as a *pied-à-terre*. At the foot of the cottage a little garden at the back leads to a small ornamental edifice with reed roofing and an "ancient" flight of steps: the Queen's Boudoir including a salon and a cloakroom. Behind all these, besides a series of enclosed flower and vegetable gardens often lined with bowers, lay several cottages housing service areas such as a *rechauffoir* and the servant's and footmen's quarters.

The illusion of country life

Within these ornamental cottages Marie-Antoinette lived a life of leisure that she believed close to Nature. One enjoyed aristocratic entertainment such as gaming, music, dance and conversation surrounded by luxurious interiors: sculpted wood panels (which unfortunately no longer exist) painted in pale, luminous colours – the Queen loved pastel colours –, highlighted with gilding. The Queen's small circle of friends indulged in fresh products from the Hamlet as well as milk from the neighbouring farm. A Dairy Shop was constructed, its interior entirely lined with white marble; there, one could savour fresh milk, cream and cheeses manufactured at the dairy factory nearby (located opposite the shop it has since been destroyed). A porcelain service was specially ordered from the Sevres Royal manufacture (the Dairy Shop was however not as opulent as that of Rambouillet chateau, also built for the Queen).

❋ *View of the Queen's Boudoir*

View of the Farm with, in the foreground, a cultivated hillside

❀ *Exterior view of the Dairy Shop*

Jean-Jacques
Lagrenée le Jeune (1739-1821)
***Milk bowl (known as "jatte
téton"*** – nipple basin***), set on
a tripod base, designed for
Marie-Antoinette's Dairy Shop
in Rambouillet***, 1788
Hard-paste porcelain,
Sèvres manufacture,
12.5 x 12.2 x 13.3 cm
Sèvres, Cité de la céramique

The fishery tower looking onto the artificial lake was used to stock the fishing equipment. The Queen would fish carp and pike with her children and friends including of course Madame de Polignac who was always eager to take part in such pleasant activities. The fishery tower was named the Malborough Tower, a very anglophile homage paid to the great British General who had died in 1722 and was celebrated by a popular song *"Malborough s'en va-t-en guerre"* that the Dauphin's wet-nurse, *Madame Poitrine* (Madame Chest) would sing. Marie-Antoinette would also often play the tune on her harpsichord. From the top of the tower it was possible to communicate by signals with the chateau. Another country activity enjoyed by the Queen was boating on the lake and river. Marie-Antoinette and her intimate friends would settle on simply decorated but comfortable rowboats. A beautiful watermill brightened up with potted flowers was set on the opposite bank of the lake. Its wheels served to grind grain, and nearby, a small wash-shed was used by the farmers from the Hamlet.

Inside the Dairy Shop

❋ *View of the Farm*

An ideal farm

In addition to the Hamlet, the construction of a farm was launched in 1784. A farmer, his wife and children were lodged in the facilities which also included a stable, a farmyard and a dovecote. The neighbouring hillsides were covered by pastures and fields of barley, oats, buckwheat, alfalfa, clover and flax. Also, a full collection of particularly well groomed animals – chickens, roosters, geese, pigs, sheep, goats, cows, bulls, calves and a donkey, a billy goat and a beautifully white Suisse horse– completed the farm. Though they were not all decorated with bows, like the little sheep that have often been associated with Marie-Antoinette playacting a fancy shepherdess, the Queen could not envision Nature other than absolutely clean and sweet smelling. She enjoyed wandering around the somewhat artificial farm with her children, petting the animals, eating fruit from the orchards and gathering wild flowers. At the Hamlet she felt as close as possible to an ideal life: surrounded by her children (the dauphin's poor health required good quality country air), dressed in a simple white dress (nearly transparent), hair untied and without face powder under a large straw hat. Because of this "Rousseauist" image of a modern mother who wishes to live without constraints, in harmony with a pastoral Nature, Marie-Antoinette is a pre-Romantic figure. Truly, the Hamlet and the gardens of Petit Trianon are a commemoration of the last queen of Versailles.

François Dumont (1751-1831)
Portrait of Marie-Antoinette, her daughter and her second son, 1790
Painted ivory, 19.5 x 14.3 cm
Paris, Louvre Museum

The last Chateau

Financial difficulties (the State was on the verge of bankruptcy) and political instability (the ideas of Enlightenment questioned the very principles of absolute monarchy) forced Louis XVI to convene the Estates General in May 1789. The deputies, in particular those of the Third Estate, arrived at Versailles in the hopes that profound revisions of the monarchy would be undertaken. Louis XVI and his ministers, however, were only expecting a vote on additional taxes. When the Revolution hit Versailles, Marie-Antoinette realised how unpopular she was, how much she was hated and blamed for all the kingdom's ailments especially the disastrous financial situation of the country. When the Deputies walked around "Madame Deficit's" private domain and asked to visit the theatre, they were quite surprised to see the walls were not covered with emeralds and other precious stones… Though the summer of 1789 was relatively quiet (just a few hours after the Bastille fell, the Polignacs, the Count d'Artois and a great deal of courtesans emigrated), towards autumn accusations against royal authority and the Queen became more and more radical. On 5th and 6th October 1789, the Parisians marched on Versailles to demand that the capital be supplied with shipments of grain; furthermore they wanted the "baker, the baker's wife and the baker's boy" in Paris, so that they could be put under the Revolution's close surveillance. During the night of 5th to 6th October, the insurgents entered the palace. They reached without much hindrance the Queen's State Rooms. A personal guard barely had the time to warn the Queen and her ladies of the armed attack (he was killed, beheaded, and his head planted on a pike). Marie-Antoinette threw on a robe and fled her bedchamber

❊ View of the Marble Courtyard showing the King's Bedchamber balcony where, in the morning of 6th October 1789, Marie-Antoinette appeared to satisfy the angry crowd of Parisians

Élisabeth Vigée-Le Brun
(1755-1842)
Marie-Antoinette seated, wearing a white dress and blue overcoat, with a book in hand, 1788
Oil on canvas, 271 x 195 cm

Anonymous
The terrible night from 5th to 6th October 1789,
18th century
Engraving, 14.2 x 8.5 cm

❋ *View of the bedchamber door through which Marie-Antoinette escaped during the night of 5th to 6th October 1789*

through a door located between her bed and a monumental jewellery cabinet by Schwerdfeger. She went to her Private Rooms and used the corridors and mezzanine stairways only used by herself – and her servants – which ran behind her official apartments, to finally reach the King's official bedchamber. There she found Louis XVI, her children, members of the royal family (among which the Count and Countess de Provence), some Ministers and the Marquis de La Fayette who had been appointed Commander of the National Guard since July. The crowd demanded that the King come out onto the balcony. When he appeared he was acclaimed; when he announced he agreed to leave Versailles for Paris the crowd applauded enthusiastically. The throng, up in arms, then demanded the Queen appear. Courageously she stepped out with her eldest, Madame Royale, and the Dauphin. The people cried out that she shouldn't hide behind her children. Voices rose, the "Austrian", the "whore" should be killed. Marie-Antoinette replied with a majestic curtsy, consequently she too was applauded. In the early afternoon, the royal family was loaded onto a coach; the last Marie-Antoinette would ever see of their ancestor Louis XIV's palace was her ransacked State bedchamber. It is said her Official bed had been lacerated by pikes and knives. The only Queen that ever really reigned over Versailles, Marie-Antoinette will have endured its constraints and tedium, taken part in its luxury, pleasures, and scandals to finally witness, within the chateau walls, the eruption of a young Revolution.

Dates and Events

Historical and political events are highlighted with italic font,
those relating to Marie-Antoinette's personal life are underlined and in bold font.

2nd November 1755 Birth of Archduchess Marie-Antoinette in Vienna.

1756-1763 *Seven Year War.*

19th April 1770 Proxy marriage of the Dauphin of France and the Archduchess Marie-Antoinette.

21st April 1770 The young Dauphine of France leaves Vienna.

16th May 1770 Wedding celebration for the Dauphin Louis Auguste and the Dauphine Marie-Antoinette at the Royal Chapel, Versailles.

16th - 30th May 1770 Nuptial festivities given at Versailles and in Paris to honour the heir-apparent and his new wife.

10 May 1774 *Death of Louis XV. Louis XVI becomes King.*

11 May 1774 The Queen meets the milliner Rose Bertin.

15 August 1774 Louis XVI gives Petit Trianon to Marie-Antoinette.

1774 The *libelle* "The Break of Day" attacking Marie-Antoinette is published.

11 June 1775 *Louis XVI is crowned in Reims.*

1777-1778 Construction of the temple of Love on the grounds.

February 1778 *France is officially engaged in the American war of Independence against England.*

19 December 1778 Birth of Marie Thérèse Charlotte known as "Madame Royale".

1778-1779 Construction of the Queen's Theatre at Trianon and, in the gardens, the Belvedere.

1779 First remodelling of the Queen's Private Rooms (*cabinets intérieurs*), notably the *Cabinet doré* located in the main body of Versailles palace.

1781 Works launched in the Meridian Room.

22 October 1781 Birth of the heir-apparent, Louis Joseph de France.

1782 Madame of Polignac becomes Governess of the Children of France.

August 1783 Élisabeth Vigée-Le Brun's portrait, *Marie-Antoinette wearing a robe described as "en Gaulle"*, causes a scandal at the Salon du Louvre and is replaced by *Marie-Antoinette à la rose*.

September 1783 *End of the American war of Independence with the signature of the Treaty of Paris.*

1783 Replacement of the wood panelling in the *Cabinet doré*, launch of the works for the ground floor apartment looking onto the Marble Courtyard; launch of the construction of the Hamlet.

27 March 1785 Birth of Louis Charles Duke of Normandy.

August 1785 Performance of the *Barber of Seville* by Beaumarchais at the Queen's Theatre by the Company of Lords.

August 1785-May 1786 *The Affair of the Queen's Necklace.*

9 July 1786 Birth of Marie-Sophie Béatrice de France.

19 June 1787 Death of Marie-Sophie Béatrice de France.

August 1787 Élisabeth Vigée-Le Brun's painting, *Marie-Antoinette and her Children*, is exhibited at the Salon du Louvre.

November-December 1788 *Second Assembly of Notables takes place at Versailles.*

5 May 1789 *Opening of the Estates General in the Salle des Menus-Plaisirs at Versailles.*

4 June 1789 Death of the Dauphin Louis Joseph de France.

20 June 1789 *The Tennis Court Oath.*

14 July 1789 *The fall of the Bastille prison.*

16 July 1789 Most of the court including the Polignac's and the Count of Artois emigrate; the Duchess of Tourzel is named Governess of the Children of France.

4 August 1789 at night *Abolition of privileges.*

26 August 1789 *The Declaration of the Rights of Man and the Citizen are voted by the National Assembly.*

1st October 1789 *Banquet for the Flanders regiment in the Royal Opera House at Versailles.*

5-6 October 1789 *Parisian women and men march on Versailles to bring back to Paris "the baker, the baker's wife and the baker's son".*

6 October 1789 The royal family leaves Versailles forever (they set up at the Tuileries Palace in Paris).

June 1791 Flight of the royal family stopped at Varennes-en-Argonne.

10 August 1792 *Fall of the monarchy;* the royal family is incarcerated at the Temple Tower in Paris.

December 1792-January 1793 Trial of Louis XVI alias Capet.

21st January 1793 *Execution of Louis Capet on Revolution Square.*

Night of 1st to 2nd August 1793 The widow Capet is transferred to the Conciergerie Prison.

14-16 October Trial of the widow Capet.

16 October 1793 Execution of the widow Capet on Revolution Square.

Selected Bibliography

ON THE CHÂTEAU OF VERSAILLES

VERLET, Pierre (1961). *Le château de Versailles*. Paris: Librairie Arthème Fayard.

LEVRON, Jacques (1965). *La Cour de Versailles aux XVIIe et XVIIIe siècles*. Paris: Éditions Hachette.

BABELON, Jean-Pierre, BAJOU, Thierry, CONSTANS, Claire, POUGETOUX, Alain, SALMON, Xavier (1996), *L'ABCdaire du château de Versailles*. Paris: Flammarion.

SOLNON, Jean-François (1997), *Histoire de Versailles*. Paris: Perrin.

NEWTON, William Ritchey (2000), *L'Espace du Roi. La cour de France au château de Versailles, 1682-1789*. Paris: Fayard ; (2008), *Derrière la façade. Vivre au château de Versailles au XVIIIe siècle*. Paris: Perrin; (2011), *Versailles, côté jardins. Splendeurs et misères, de Louis XIV à la Révolution*. Paris: Tallandier.

LACAILLE, Frédéric (2012), *Versailles. 400 ans d'histoire*. Versailles-Paris: château de Versailles-Gallimard.

ON MARIE-ANTOINETTE

GONCOURT, Edmond and Jules de (1858), *Histoire de Marie-Antoinette*. Paris: Firmin-Didot.

NOLHAC, Pierre de (1889), *La Reine Marie-Antoinette*. Paris; (1889), *Le Château de Versailles au temps de Marie-Antoinette*. Paris; (1890), *Les Consignes de Marie-Antoinette au Petit Trianon*. Paris; (1896), *La Dauphine Marie-Antoinette*. Paris; (1924), *Le Trianon de Marie-Antoinette*. Paris: Calmann-Lévy; (1929), *Autour de la Reine*. Paris; (1932), *Marie-Antoinette à Versailles*. Paris: Flammarion.

ZWEIG, Stefan (1932), *Marie Antoinette: The Portrait of an Average Woman*. Leipzig: Insel-Verlag.

CASTELOT, André (1953), *Marie-Antoinette*. Paris: Amiot-Dumont.

CHALON, Jean (1988), *Chère Marie-Antoinette*. Paris: Perrin.

THOMAS, Chantal (1989), *La Reine scélérate. Marie-Antoinette dans les pamphlets*. Paris: Seuil; (2002), *Les Adieux à la Reine*. Paris: Seuil; (2003), *La Lectrice-adjointe. Suivi de Marie-Antoinette et le théâtre*. Paris: Mercure de France.

LEVER, Évelyne (1991), *Marie-Antoinette*. Paris: Fayard; (2000), *Marie-Antoinette. La dernière reine*. Paris: Gallimard; (2005), *Marie-Antoinette. Correspondance (1770-1793)*. Paris: Tallandier; (2007), *Marie-Antoinette. Un destin brisé*. Paris: Rmn.

FRASER, Antonia (2001), *Marie Antoinette*. London: Wedenfeld & Nicolson.

BERTIÈRE, Simone (2002), *Marie-Antoinette l'insoumise*. Paris: Éditions de Fallois.

SAPORI, Michèle (2003), *Rose Bertin, Ministre des Modes de Marie-Antoinette*. Paris: Institut français de la Mode-Éditions du Regard; (2010), *Rose Bertin, couturière de Marie-Antoinette*. Versailles-Paris: château de Versailles-Perrin.

DE FEYDEAU, Élisabeth (2004), *Jean-Louis Fargeon, parfumeur de Marie-Antoinette*. Versailles-Paris: château de Versailles-Perrin.

GOETZ, Adrien (2005), *Le Style Marie-Antoinette*. Paris: Assouline.

DUPRAT, Annie (2006), *Marie-Antoinette. La reine dévoilée*. Paris: Perrin.

BERLY, Cécile (2006), *Marie-Antoinette et ses biographes. Histoire d'une écriture de la Révolution française*. Paris: L'Harmattan; (2010), *Marie-Antoinette*, coauthored by Jean-Clément MARTIN. Paris: Citadelles & Mazenod; (2012), *La Reine scandaleuse. Idées reçues sur Marie-Antoinette*. Paris: Le Cavalier Bleu.

CRAVERI, Benedetta (2008), *Marie-Antoinette et le scandale du collier*. Paris: Gallimard.

HIGONNET, Patrice (2011), *La Gloire et l'échafaud. Vie et destin de l'architecte de Marie-Antoinette*. Paris: Vendémiaire.

EXHIBITION CATALOGUES

Les Atours de la Reine (2001). Paris: Centre historique des Archives nationales.

Marie-Antoinette à Versailles. Le goût d'une reine (2005). Bordeaux-Paris: musée des Arts décoratifs de Bordeaux-Somogy.

Gazette des atours de Marie-Antoinette (2006). Paris: Archives nationales-Rmn.

ARIZZOLI-CLÉMENTEL, Pierre, SALMON, Xavier (supervised by) (2008), *Marie-Antoinette*. Paris: Rmn.

Selected Filmography

RENOIR, Jean (1937), *La Marseillaise*. France.
VAN DYKE, Woodbridge Strong, and DUVIVIER, Julien (1938),
Marie-Antoinette (film inspired by Stefan ZWEIG's biography).
United States of America.
L'HERBIER, Maurice (1945), *L'Affaire du collier de la reine*. France.
GUITRY, Sacha (1953), *Si Versailles m'était conté*. France.
DELANNOY, Jean (1955), *Marie-Antoinette*. France.
DEMY, Jacques (1978), *Lady Oscar*. France-Japan.
Lady Oscar (1979) (cartoon film inspired by the manga
La Rose de Versailles by Riyoko Ikeda). Japan.
ENRICO, Robert, and HEFFRON, Richard T. (1989),
*La Révolution française. Les années Lumières. Les années
terribles*. France, Italy, Canada, Germany, United Kingdom.
GRANIER-DEFERRE, Pierre (1993), *Marie-Antoinette*.
Le procès. France.
COPPOLA, Sofia (2006), *Marie-Antoinette*.
United States of America.
JACQUOT, Benoît (2012), *Les Adieux à la reine*. France.

❋ Norma Shearer in the film by Woodbridge Strong Van Dyke and Julien Duvivier ❋ Michèle Morgan in the film by Jean Delanno
❋ Diane Kruger in the film by Benoît Jacquot ❋ Kirsten Dunst in the film by Sofia Coppola

pages 16-17: *close-up of the tapestry in the Queen's Bedchamber*
pages 28-29: *close-up of the tapestry in the* Cabinet du Billard
pages 56-57: *ceiling of the Belvedere painted by Jean-Jacques Lagrenée le Jeune (1739-1821)*

The author wishes to thank Mathias Le Galic for his vigilant proofreading.

Unless otherwise stated, all of the works reproduced are housed at the national museum of the Châteaux of Versailles and Trianon.

PHOTOGRAPHY CREDITS

Archives Alinari (dist. Rmn-GP)/Finsiel/Alinari: p. 42b; Artlys/ Sophie Lloyd: cover, p. 1, 2, 5, 6, 8, 16-17, 27, 32tl, 32br, 35, 36-37, 41l, 41r, 42t, 43, 45, 46, 47, 48, 49t, 50t, 51, 52, 53, 56-57, 60t, 61, 62, 64, 65t, 65b, 68, 69, 72-73, 74, 75l, 75r, 77b, 78, 79, 81, 82-83, 93, 94, 95, 96, 98, 99, 101, 102, 107; BnF (dist. Rmn-GP)/image BnF: p. 91; BPK (dist. Rmn-GP)/image BPK: p. 58; château de Versailles (dist. Rmn-GP)/D.R.: p. 33l, 66b, 70t; château de Versailles (dist. Rmn-GP)/Jean-Marc Manaï: backcover, p. 4, 21, 22, 31, 32tr, 40, 66t, 67b; château de Versailles (dist. Rmn-GP)/Christian Milet: p. 19, 32bl, 33r, 59, 67t, 97, 100t; Columbia/American Zoetrope/Sony/ The Kobal Collection: p. 111; De Agostini Picture Library/A. Dagli Orti/The Bridgeman Art Library: p. 92; D.R.: p. 71; Gibe/ Franco/Londres/Gaumont/The Kobal Collection: p. 110m; GMT Productions/The Kobal Collection: p. 110r; MGM/The Kobal Collection/Laszlo Willinger: p. 110l; Musée lorrain/Nancy/G. Mangin: p. 70b; Rmn-GP (château de Blérancourt)/Michel Urtado: p. 60b; Rmn-GP (château de Versailles)/Daniel Arnaudet: p. 20l, 25, 63l, 80; Rmn-GP (château de Versailles)/Daniel Arnaudet/Gérard Blot: p. 85; Rmn-GP (château de Versailles)/Michèle Bellot: p. 49b; Rmn-GP (château de Versailles)/Gérard Blot: p. 3, 14, 18, 20m, 20r, 23, 28-29, 30, 33m, 34l, 34r, 38l, 38r, 39, 44, 55l, 55r, 63r, 76, 77t, 84, 86, 87, 88, 105, 106; Rmn-GP (château de Versailles)/D.R.: p. 90; Rmn-GP (château de Versailles)/Christian Jean/Jean Schormans: p. 104; Rmn-GP (château de Versailles)/Thierry Ollivier: p. 50b; Rmn-GP (château de Versailles)/Jean Popovitch: p. 26 ; Rmn-GP (château de Versailles)/Franck Raux: p. 7, 67m; Rmn-GP (Cité de la céramique, Sèvres)/Martine Beck-Coppola: p. 100b; Rmn-GP (domaine de Chantilly)/Harry Bréjat: p. 24; Rmn-GP (musée du Louvre)/ Michèle Bellot: p. 103.

Établissement public du château, du musée et du domaine national de Versailles

Jean-Vincent Bacquart, head of the Publishing Department
Marie Leimbacher, publishing manager, assisted by Anne Déon and Marie-Astrid Pourchet

Éditions Artlys

Editorial supervision
Séverine Cuzin-Schulte

Editorial coordination
Lucile Desmoulins

PAO
Catherine Enault

Production
Pierre Kegels

Translation
Laurette Tassin

Graphic Design
Montag, Juliane Cordes and Corinne Dury

Photoengraving
Axiome

Printing
Timedian

Printed on March 2013 in Villejust
Legal deposit : April 2013